This book has been presented to

_____

by

_____

in the hope that they will treasure
our family history.

Date

_____

Special Message

_____

_____

_____

OUR HISTORY

A KEEPSAKE

The Story of Our Family

OUR
HISTORY
A KEEPSAKE

The Story of
Our Family

ROCK
POINT
QUARTOKNOWS.COM

Inspiring | Educating | Creating | Entertaining

Brimming with creative inspiration, how-to projects, and useful information to enrich your everyday life, Quarto Knows is a favorite destination for those pursuing their interests and passions. Visit our site and dig deeper with our books into your area of interest: Quarto Creates, Quarto Cooks, Quarto Homes, Quarto Lives, Quarto Drives, Quarto Explores, Quarto Gifts, or Quarto Kids.

Text by Jennifer Boudinot
Illustrations by Becca Stadtlander
Design by Rachael Cronin

MIX
Paper from
responsible sources
FSC® C016973

CONTENTS

Introduction

HOW TO USE THIS BOOK

Knowing who our family was reveals part of who we are.

Because so much of a person is determined by what came before, this special keepsake gives you a unique opportunity to share with your young family members the important aspects of who you are, how you were raised, how you raised your own children, what's important to you, how hard you worked, what your values are, and much more. If you're a Mom or Dad sit down with your parents and in-laws and encourage them to share their memories, creating a wonderful family history for your child or children. Inside, you'll find three different sections:

1. A family tree
2. Interview sections for detailed information about both paternal and maternal grandparents
3. A shorter interview section for important family members and close family friends

Give the book to each grandparent and other relatives to fill out or ask them the questions yourself. However you decide to do it, make sure to take your time. It should be fun, so keep it that way! There are many questions inside these pages so the book can be filled out over a few sessions. If you find some questions hard to answer, simply skip them, or answer them later, if you wish.

The things you learn about the people you love—from your grandmother's favorite food to your uncle's funny story about your dad when he was a kid—will become cherished memories.

Helping your loved ones understand where they came from is a gift that they will have forever!

All about the Owner

Name
_____

Birthdate (include time and place)
_____
_____

Address
_____
_____

Favorite Food
_____

Favorite Season
_____

Favorite TV Show
_____

Favorite Movie
_____

Favorite Book
_____

Favorite Color
_____

Favorite Things to Do
_____
_____
_____
_____
_____
_____
_____

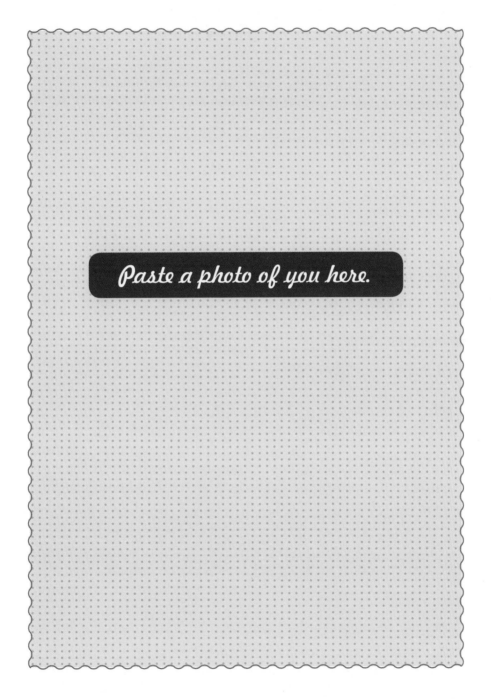

Paste a photo of you here.

Our Family Tree

Dad's Name

_____

Birthdate

_____

Birthplace

_____

Mom's Name

_____

Birthdate

_____

Birthplace

_____

Date of Marriage

_____

Place of Marriage

_____

_____

_____

_____

Our Children's Names and Birthdates

_____

_____

_____

_____

_____

_____

Dad's Parents

Mother's Name

_____

Birthdate and Birthplace

_____

Father's Name

_____

Birthdate and Birthplace

_____

Marriage Place and Date

_____

Children's Names

_____

_____

Mom's Parents

Mother's Name

_____

Birthdate and Birthplace

_____

Father's Name

_____

Birthdate and Birthplace

_____

Marriage Place and Date

_____

Children's Names

_____

_____

Dad's Paternal Grandparents

Grandfather's Name

_____

Birthdate and Birthplace

_____

Grandmother's Name

_____

Birthdate and Birthplace

_____

Marriage Place and Date

_____

_____

Mom's Paternal Grandparents

Grandfather's Name

_____

Birthdate and Birthplace

_____

Grandmother's Name

_____

Birthdate and Birthplace

_____

Marriage Place and Date

_____

_____

Dad's Maternal Grandparents

Grandfather's Name

_____

Birthdate and Birthplace

_____

Grandmother's Name

_____

Birthdate and Birthplace

_____

Marriage Place and Date

_____

_____

Mom's Maternal Grandparents

Grandfather's Name

_____

Birthdate and Birthplace

_____

Grandmother's Name

_____

Birthdate and Birthplace

_____

Marriage Place and Date

_____

_____

Our Family Tree

Dad's Great- and Great-Great-Grandparents

Paternal Great-Grandfather's Name

_____

Birth/Death Dates

_____

Paternal Great-Grandmother's Name

_____

Birth/Death Dates

_____

Maternal Great-Grandfather's Name

_____

Birth/Death Dates

_____

Maternal Great-Grandmother's Name

_____

Birth/Death Date

_____

Paternal Great-Great-Grandfather's Name

_____

Birth/Death Dates

_____

Paternal Great-Great-Grandmother's Name

_____

Birth/Death Dates

_____

Maternal Great-Great-Grandfather's Name

_____

Birth/Death Dates

_____

Maternal Great-Great-Grandmother's Name

_____

Birth/Death Dates

_____

Mom's Great- and Great-Great-Grandparents

Paternal Great-Grandfather's Name

_____

Birth/Death Dates

_____

Paternal Great-Grandmother's Name

_____

Birth/Death Dates

_____

Maternal Great-Grandfather's Name

_____

Birth/Death Dates

_____

Maternal Great-Grandmother's Name

_____

Birth/Death Dates

_____

Paternal Great-Great-Grandfather's Name

_____

Birth/Death Dates

_____

Paternal Great-Great-Grandmother's Name

_____

Birth/Death Dates

_____

Maternal Great-Great-Grandfather's Name

_____

Birth/Death Dates

_____

Maternal Great-Great-Grandmother's Name

_____

Birth/Death Dates

_____

Maternal Grandparents Interview

Couple's Names

_____

Meeting

When did you meet each other? How did you meet?

_____
_____
_____

How old were each of you?

_____

What did you do on your first date?

_____
_____

Was there a moment when you knew he or she was "the one"?

_____
_____

What were some of your favorite things to do as a couple when you first met?

_____
_____

Your Wedding

What is the story of your engagement?

_____
_____

What date did you get married?

_____

Where was your wedding held?

_____

Who was in your bridal party?

_____

Where did you go on your honeymoon?

_____

What do you think makes a relationship last?

_____
_____

Your Children

What are the full names and birthdates of your children?

_____

_____

_____

_____

When did you first begin to think about having children of your own?

_____

_____

Where did you live when your children were growing up?

_____

_____

What are the stories of how your children were born?

_____

_____

_____

_____

_____

_____

How did you spend summers when your children were growing up?

_____

_____

_____

What did you usually do to celebrate your children's birthdays?

_____

_____

_____

What was your favorite thing about raising children?

_____

_____

_____

What was the hardest thing about raising children?

_____

_____

_____

Maternal Grandmother Interview

Name

_____

Likes and Dislikes

Favorite color

_____

Favorite animals

_____

Least favorite animals (or insects)

_____

Favorite food

_____

Favorite desserts

_____

Favorite snacks

_____

Favorite beverages

_____

Least favorite food and beverages

_____

Favorite movies

_____

_____

Favorite TV shows

_____

_____

Favorite actors and actresses

_____

_____

Favorite authors and books

_____

_____

Favorite musicians or bands

_____

Favorite season of the year

_____

Least favorite season of the year

_____

Your Parents

What were your parents' full names?

_____

_____

Where were your parents born and where did they grow up?

_____

_____

What is your family's ethnic background and where are your ancestors from?

_____

What languages were spoken in your home?

_____

How would you describe your mother?

_____

_____

_____

How would you describe your father?

_____

_____

_____

_____

Did your parents ever tell you any stories about growing up?

_____

_____

_____

_____

What recollections do you have about each of your grandparents?

_____

_____

_____

Do you remember your parents having particular interests or passions?

_____

What did your mother teach you about life?

_____

_____

What did your father teach you about life?

_____

_____

Religion and Spirituality

What is your religion?

_____

Did religion play a big part in your family's life growing up?

_____

_____

_____

What do you love the most about your place of worship?

_____

_____

_____

What aspects of your faith speak to you and impassion you the most?

_____

_____

Do you have a special prayer you often say?

_____

_____

Do you have a particular prayer you like to say before meals?

_____

_____

How has religion or spirituality enriched your life?

_____

_____

What kind of advice would you give about your faith or spirituality?

_____

_____

_____

Favorite Religious Text
Do you have any favorite sacred passages? Write them below.

_____

_____

_____

_____

_____

Your Best Stories

Write some of your favorite stories here.
What's the funniest thing that's ever happened to you?
Do you find yourself telling the same anecdote time and time again?

_____

_____

_____

_____

_____

_____

_____

_____

_____

_____

_____

_____

_____

_____

Pets

Are you a: ☐ cat person   ☐ dog person   ☐ fish person   ☐ none   ☐ other: _____

Do you think having a pet is important? Why or why not?

_____

_____

What is the oldest pet you've ever had?

_____

_____

Have you ever taught a pet any special tricks? Which pet and what were they?

_____

_____

List your favorite pets you've had.

Name   **Type of animal**

_____

Boy/Girl   Description

_____

Where did you get him/her?

_____

How old were you when you had him/her?

_____

Special recollections

_____

_____

_____

Name   **Type of animal**

_____

Boy/Girl   Description

_____

Where did you get him/her?

_____

How old were you when you had him/her?

_____

Special recollections

_____

_____

Growing Up

What is the date of your birth? Where were you born?

_____

Do you know any stories about your birth?

_____
_____

Where did you grow up?

_____

What are the names and birthdates of your brothers and sisters?

_____
_____
_____

Did you have a nickname? If so, how did you get it or who gave it to you?

_____
_____

Did you have any chores or family responsibilities? What were they?

_____
_____

Did you get an allowance? If so, how much?

_____
_____

Do you remember how you usually spent it?

_____
_____

How did you spend your summers as a child?

_____
_____

What did you usually do to celebrate your birthday?

_____
_____

Did you have any cousins or other relatives who were particularly special to you?

_____
_____

Do you have a memory of a favorite family trip or event?

_____
_____

Childhood Favorites

What was your favorite ice cream flavor?

_____

What was your favorite meal or snack?

_____

What were some of your favorite childhood toys?

_____

_____

What were your favorite books?

_____

_____

What were your favorite TV or radio shows?

_____

_____

What were your favorite movies?

_____

_____

Who were your favorite celebrities?

_____

_____

Who were your favorite musical performers?

_____

_____

How did you listen to music?

_____

Who were some of your best friends as a child?

_____

What were your favorite games to play with friends?

_____

_____

Teenage Years

What high school(s) did you attend?

_____

What did you like about high school?

_____

_____

What did you dislike about high school?

_____

_____

Which teachers made an impression on you, and why?

_____

_____

How did you get to and from school?

_____

What after-school activities did you participate in?

_____

_____

Did you have a job as a teenager? What did you do and how much were you paid?

_____

_____

What did you do when you returned home from school?

_____

Who were some of your best friends as a teenager?

_____

What did you do when spending time with friends?

_____

What were some of the fashion fads of the time, and did you follow them?

_____

What kind of hairstyle did you have?

_____

What stores do you remember shopping at as a teen?

_____

_____

Did you have any teenage rebellions?

_____

What were your favorite things to eat as a teenager?

_____

What were your favorite books?

_____

_____

What were some of your favorite movies?

_____

_____

What were some of your favorite TV or radio programs?

_____

_____

What were your favorite bands or musical performers?

_____

_____

Who were your favorite celebrities?

_____

_____

What were your favorite sports teams and who were your favorite athletes?

_____

_____

What were your hopes and fears about college or growing up?

_____

_____

When you graduated high school, did you feel like an adult?

_____

_____

The Times

What is your generation called?

_____

What is the first major news event you remember hearing about as a child?

_____

What is a new invention or technology you remember seeing for the first time when you were young?

_____

How much did a movie ticket cost?

_____

Gallon of gas?   Burger and fries?

_____

Who was the first person you voted for president or other national office?

_____

What pivotal events in history do you remember happening, or did you witness firsthand?

_____

_____

College and Work

Where did you study after high school? When did you graduate, and what was your degree(s)?

_____
_____
_____

Who were your closest friends in college or as a young adult?

_____
_____
_____

What did you like to do together?

_____
_____
_____

Who were your favorite instructors or professors, and why?

_____
_____
_____

If you didn't pursue a formal education, what was your training and experience?

_____
_____
_____

What was dating like when you were a young adult?

_____
_____
_____

What do you consider your occupation to be?

_____

Do you feel like you "fell into" your career, or did it take a lot of planning?

_____
_____

What was your first professional job? How old were you, and how much did you make?

_____
_____
_____

Were you ever forced to make a big change in your career?

_____

_____

_____

_____

What was it, and how did you overcome it?

_____

_____

_____

What was the most favorite job you've ever had? Why?

_____

_____

_____

What was the most lucrative job you've ever had?

_____

_____

_____

What was the worst job you've ever had? Why?

_____

_____

_____

_____

A Wild Night
Did you ever experience a wild night as a young adult? Describe it below.

_____

_____

_____

_____

_____

_____

_____

_____

_____

Holidays

What is your favorite holiday, and why?

_____

_____

Did you have any special Halloween traditions with your child(ren)?

_____

_____

What is your favorite Halloween candy?

_____

Growing up, where did you usually spend the holidays, and with whom?

_____

_____

When your children were growing up, where did you spend the holidays, and with whom?

_____

_____

What are your favorite holiday dishes?

_____

_____

What are your favorite parts of the holiday season?

_____

_____

What are your favorite or most treasured holiday decorations?

_____

_____

What are your favorite holiday songs?

_____

_____

When you were growing up, how did your family celebrate Christmas or Hanukkah, and with whom?

_____

_____

_____

When your children were growing up, how did your family celebrate Christmas or Hanukkah, and with whom?

_____

_____

_____

Does your family have any special dishes it makes for Christmas or Hanukkah?

_____

_____

_____

What was the most memorable New Year's Eve you ever spent?

_____

_____

_____

What are your Easter or Passover traditions?

_____

_____

_____

_____

Are there any other holidays (religious or otherwise) that you regularly celebrated? How did you celebrate?

_____

_____

_____

_____

A Favorite Recipe
Write your family's special holiday recipe here.

_____

_____

_____

_____

_____

For Future Generations

What You've Learned

What do you think are the most important things in life?

_____

_____

_____

Is there an incident or a time in your life when you've felt blessed by extraordinary luck?

_____

_____

_____

Is there anything people might not know about you, that you wish they knew?

_____

_____

Is there anything you wish you'd done differently in your life? What?

_____

_____

What issues do you wish people would care more about?

_____

_____

_____

What do people get too riled up about?

_____

_____

_____

What are the most important characteristics in a good friend?

_____

_____

What is the most important way you can be a good friend to others?

_____

_____

_____

What is important to remember about family in general?

_____

_____

Do you have any hopes for future generations?

_____

_____

How do you hope we will remember you?

_____

_____

What do you love about our family?

_____

_____

In what ways is the owner of this book similar to his or her parents? Different?

_____

_____

_____

Paste a photo of us here.

Maternal Grandfather Interview

Name
_____

Likes and Dislikes

Favorite color
_____

Favorite animals
_____

Least favorite animals (or insects)
_____

Favorite food
_____

Favorite desserts
_____

Favorite snacks
_____

Favorite beverages
_____

Least favorite food and beverages
_____

Favorite movies
_____
_____

Favorite TV shows
_____
_____

Favorite actors and actresses
_____
_____

Favorite authors and books
_____
_____

Favorite musicians or bands
_____

Favorite season of the year
_____

Least favorite season of the year
_____

Your Parents

What were your parents' full names?

_____

_____

Where were your parents born and where did they grow up?

_____

_____

What is your family's ethnic background and where are your ancestors from?

_____

What languages were spoken in your home?

_____

How would you describe your mother?

_____

_____

_____

How would you describe your father?

_____

_____

_____

_____

Did your parents ever tell you any stories about growing up?

_____

_____

_____

_____

What recollections do you have about each of your grandparents?

_____

_____

_____

Do you remember your parents having particular interests or passions?

_____

What did your mother teach you about life?

_____

_____

What did your father teach you about life?

_____

_____

Religion and Spirituality

What is your religion?

_____

Did religion play a big part in your family's life growing up?

_____

_____

What do you love the most about your place of worship?

_____

What aspects of your faith speak to you and impassion you the most?

_____

Do you have a special prayer you often say?

_____

Do you have a particular prayer you like to say before meals?

_____

How has religion or spirituality enriched your life?

_____

_____

What kind of advice would you give about your faith or spirituality?

_____

_____

Favorite Religious Text
Do you have any favorite sacred passages? Write them below.

_____

_____

_____

_____

Your Best Stories

Write some of your favorite stories here.
What's the funniest thing that's ever happened to you?
Do you find yourself telling the same anecdote time and time again?

Pets

Are you a: ☐ cat person   ☐ dog person   ☐ fish person   ☐ none   ☐ other: _____

Do you think having a pet is important? Why or why not?

_____

_____

What is the oldest pet you've ever had?

_____

_____

Have you ever taught a pet any special tricks? Which pet and what were they?

_____

_____

List your favorite pets you've had.

Name _____ **Type of animal** _____

Boy/Girl _____ Description _____

Where did you get him/her? _____

How old were you when you had him/her? _____

Special recollections _____

_____

_____

Name _____ **Type of animal** _____

Boy/Girl _____ Description _____

Where did you get him/her? _____

How old were you when you had him/her? _____

Special recollections _____

_____

_____

Growing Up

What is the date of your birth? Where were you born?

_____

Do you know any stories about your birth?

_____
_____
_____

Where did you grow up?

_____

What are the names and birthdates of your brothers and sisters?

_____
_____
_____

Did you have a nickname? If so, how did you get it or who gave it to you?

_____
_____

Did you have any chores or family responsibilities? What were they?

_____
_____

Did you get an allowance? If so, how much?

_____
_____

Do you remember how you usually spent it?

_____
_____

How did you spend your summers as a child?

_____
_____

What did you usually do to celebrate your birthday?

_____
_____

Did you have any cousins or other relatives who were particularly special to you?

_____
_____

Do you have a memory of a favorite family trip or event?

_____
_____

Childhood Favorites

What was your favorite ice cream flavor?

_____

What was your favorite meal or snack?

_____

_____

What were some of your favorite childhood toys?

_____

_____

_____

What were your favorite books?

_____

_____

_____

What were your favorite TV or radio shows?

_____

_____

_____

What were your favorite movies?

_____

_____

_____

Who were your favorite celebrities?

_____

_____

_____

Who were your favorite musical performers?

_____

_____

_____

How did you listen to music?

_____

_____

Who were some of your best friends as a child?

_____

_____

What were your favorite games to play with friends?

_____

_____

Teenage Years

What high school(s) did you attend?

_____

What did you like about high school?

_____

_____

What did you dislike about high school?

_____

_____

Which teachers made an impression on you, and why?

_____

_____

How did you get to and from school?

_____

What after-school activities did you participate in?

_____

Did you have a job as a teenager? What did you do and how much were you paid?

_____

_____

What did you do when you returned home from school?

_____

Who were some of your best friends as a teenager?

_____

_____

What did you do when spending time with friends?

_____

_____

What were some of the fashion fads of the time, and did you follow them?

_____

What kind of hairstyle did you have?

_____

What stores do you remember shopping at as a teen?

_____

_____

Did you have any teenage rebellions?

_____

What were your favorite things to eat as a teenager?

_____

What were your favorite books?

_____

_____

What were some of your favorite movies?

_____

_____

What were some of your favorite TV or radio programs?

_____

_____

What were your favorite bands or musical performers?

_____

_____

Who were your favorite celebrities?

_____

_____

What were your favorite sports teams and who were your favorite athletes?

_____

_____

What were your hopes and fears about college or growing up?

_____

_____

When you graduated high school, did you feel like an adult?

_____

_____

The Times

What is your generation called?

_____

What is the first major news event you remember hearing about as a child?

_____

What is a new invention or technology you remember seeing for the first time when you were young?

_____

How much did a movie ticket cost?

_____

Gallon of gas?   Burger and fries?

_____

Who was the first person you voted for president or other national office?

_____

What pivotal events in history do you remember happening, or did you witness firsthand?

_____

_____

College and Work

Where did you study after high school? When did you graduate, and what was your degree(s)?

_____
_____
_____

Who were your closest friends in college or as a young adult?

_____
_____
_____

What did you like to do together?

_____
_____
_____

Who were your favorite instructors or professors, and why?

_____
_____
_____

If you didn't pursue a formal education, what was your training and experience?

_____
_____
_____

What was dating like when you were a young adult?

_____
_____
_____

What do you consider your occupation to be?

_____
_____

Do you feel like you "fell into" your career, or did it take a lot of planning?

_____
_____
_____

What was your first professional job? How old were you, and how much did you make?

_____
_____
_____

Were you ever forced to make a big change in your career?

_____

_____

_____

What was it, and how did you overcome it?

_____

_____

What was the most favorite job you've ever had? Why?

_____

_____

What was the most lucrative job you've ever had?

_____

_____

What was the worst job you've ever had? Why?

_____

_____

_____

A Wild Night

Did you ever experience a wild night as a young adult? Describe it below.

_____

_____

_____

_____

_____

_____

_____

_____

Holidays

What is your favorite holiday, and why?

_____
_____
_____

Did you have any special Halloween traditions with your child(ren)?

_____
_____
_____

What is your favorite Halloween candy?

_____

Growing up, where did you usually spend the holidays, and with whom?

_____
_____
_____

When your children were growing up, where did you spend the holidays, and with whom?

_____
_____
_____

What are your favorite holiday dishes?

_____
_____
_____

What are your favorite parts of the holiday season?

_____
_____
_____

What are your favorite or most treasured holiday decorations?

_____
_____
_____

What are your favorite holiday songs?

_____
_____
_____

When you were growing up, how did your family celebrate Christmas or Hanukkah, and with whom?

_____

_____

_____

When your children were growing up, how did your family celebrate Christmas or Hanukkah, and with whom?

_____

_____

_____

Does your family have any special dishes it makes for Christmas or Hanukkah?

_____

_____

_____

What was the most memorable New Year's Eve you ever spent?

_____

_____

_____

What are your Easter or Passover traditions?

_____

_____

_____

Are there any other holidays (religious or otherwise) that you regularly celebrated? How did you celebrate?

_____

_____

_____

A Favorite Tradition

Write your family's special holiday tradition here.

_____

_____

_____

_____

_____

_____

For Future Generations

What do you think are the most important things in life?

_____

_____

Is there an incident or a time in your life when you've felt blessed by extraordinary luck?

_____

_____

_____

Is there anything people might not know about you, that you wish they knew?

_____

_____

Is there anything you wish you'd done differently in your life? What?

_____

_____

What issues do you wish people would care more about?

_____

_____

What do people get too riled up about?

_____

_____

What are the most important characteristics in a good friend?

_____

_____

What is the most important way you can be a good friend to others?

_____

_____

What is important to remember about family in general?

_____
_____

Do you have any hopes for future generations?

_____
_____
_____

How do you hope we will remember you?

_____
_____

What do you love about our family?

_____
_____

In what ways is the owner of this book similar to his or her parents? Different?

_____
_____
_____

Paste a photo of us here.

Paternal Grandparents Interview

Couple's Names

_____

Meeting

When did you meet each other? How did you meet?

_____

How old were each of you?

_____

What did you do on your first date?

_____

_____

Was there a moment when you knew he or she was "the one"?

_____

_____

What were some of your favorite things to do as a couple when you first met?

_____

_____

Your Wedding

What is the story of your engagement?

_____

_____

What date did you get married?

_____

Where was your wedding held?

_____

Who was in your bridal party?

_____

Where did you go on your honeymoon?

_____

What do you think makes a relationship last?

_____

_____

Your Children

What are the full names and birthdates of your children?

_____
_____
_____

When did you first begin to think about having children of your own?

_____

Where did you live when your children were growing up?

_____

What are the stories of how your children were born?

_____
_____
_____
_____

How did you spend summers when your children were growing up?

_____
_____
_____

What did you usually do to celebrate your children's birthdays?

_____
_____
_____

What was your favorite thing about raising children?

_____
_____
_____

What was the hardest thing about raising children?

_____
_____
_____
_____

Paternal Grandmother Interview

Name
_____

Likes and Dislikes

Favorite color
_____

Favorite animals
_____

Least favorite animals (or insects)
_____

Favorite food
_____

Favorite desserts
_____

Favorite snacks
_____

Favorite beverages
_____

Least favorite food and beverages
_____

Favorite movies
_____
_____

Favorite TV shows
_____

Favorite actors and actresses
_____
_____

Favorite authors and books
_____
_____

Favorite musicians or bands
_____
_____

Favorite season of the year
_____

Least favorite season of the year
_____

Your Parents

What were your parents' full names?

_____

_____

Where were your parents born and where did they grow up?

_____

_____

What is your family's ethnic background and where are your ancestors from?

_____

What languages were spoken in your home?

_____

How would you describe your mother?

_____

_____

_____

How would you describe your father?

_____

_____

_____

Did your parents ever tell you any stories about growing up?

_____

_____

_____

What recollections do you have about each of your grandparents?

_____

_____

_____

What did your mother teach you about life?

_____

_____

_____

What did your father teach you about life?

_____

_____

_____

Religion and Spirituality

What is your religion?

_____

Did religion play a big part in your family's life growing up?

_____

_____

What do you love the most about your place of worship?

_____

_____

What aspects of your faith speak to you and impassion you the most?

_____

_____

You have a special prayer you often say?

_____

_____

Do you have a particular prayer you like to say before meals?

_____

_____

How has religion or spirituality enriched your life?

_____

_____

What kind of advice would you give about your faith or spirituality?

_____

_____

Favorite Religious Text
Do you have any favorite sacred passages? Write them below.

_____

_____

_____

_____

Your Best Stories

Write some of your favorite stories here.
What's the funniest thing that's ever happened to you?
Do you find yourself telling the same anecdote time and time again?

Pets

Are you a: ☐ cat person ☐ dog person ☐ fish person ☐ none ☐ other: _____

Do you think having a pet is important? Why or why not?

_____
_____

What is the oldest pet you've ever had?

_____
_____

Have you ever taught a pet any special tricks? Which pet and what were they?

_____
_____

List your favorite pets you've had.

Name _____ **Type of animal** _____

Boy/Girl _____ Description _____

Where did you get him/her? _____

How old were you when you had him/her? _____

Special recollections _____
_____
_____
_____

Name _____ **Type of animal** _____

Boy/Girl _____ Description _____

Where did you get him/her? _____

How old were you when you had him/her? _____

Special recollections _____
_____
_____
_____

Growing Up

What is the date of your birth? Where were you born?

_____

Do you know any stories about your birth?

_____
_____
_____

Where did you grow up?

_____

What are the names and birthdates of your brothers and sisters?

_____
_____
_____

Did you have a nickname? If so, how did you get it or who gave it to you?

_____
_____

Did you have any chores or family responsibilities? What were they?

_____
_____

Did you get an allowance? If so, how much?

_____
_____

Do you remember how you usually spent it?

_____
_____

How did you spend your summers as a child?

_____
_____

What did you usually do to celebrate your birthday?

_____
_____

Did you have any cousins or other relatives who were particularly special to you?

_____
_____

Do you have a memory of a favorite family trip or event?

_____
_____

Childhood Favorites

What was your favorite ice cream flavor?

_____

What was your favorite meal or snack?

_____
_____

What were some of your favorite childhood toys?

_____
_____

What were your favorite books?

_____
_____

What were your favorite TV or radio shows?

_____
_____

What were your favorite movies?

_____
_____

Who were your favorite celebrities?

_____
_____

Who were your favorite musical performers?

_____
_____

How did you listen to music?

_____

Who were some of your best friends as a child?

_____

What were your favorite games to play with friends?

_____
_____

Teenage Years

What high school(s) did you attend?

What did you like about high school?

What did you dislike about high school?

Which teachers made an impression on you, and why?

How did you get to and from school?

What after-school activities did you participate in?

Did you have a job as a teenager? What did you do and how much were you paid?

What did you do when you returned home from school?

Who were some of your best friends as a teenager?

What did you do when spending time with friends?

What were some of the fashion fads of the time, and did you follow them?

What kind of hairstyle did you have?

What stores do you remember shopping at as a teen?

Did you have any teenage rebellions?

What were your favorite things to eat as a teenager?

What were your favorite books?

___

What were some of your favorite movies?

___

What were some of your favorite TV or radio programs?

___

What were your favorite bands or musical performers?

___

Who were your favorite celebrities?

___

What were your favorite sports teams and who were your favorite athletes?

___

What were your hopes and fears about college or growing up?

___

When you graduated high school, did you feel like an adult?

___

The Times

What is your generation called?

___

What is the first major news event you remember hearing about as a child?

___

What is a new invention or technology you remember seeing for the first time when you were young?

___

How much did a movie ticket cost?

___

Gallon of gas?   Burger and fries?

___

Who was the first person you voted for president or other national office?

___

What pivotal events in history do you remember happening, or did you witness firsthand?

___

College and Work

Where did you study after high school? When did you graduate, and what was your degree(s)?

_____

_____

_____

Who were your closest friends in college or as a young adult?

_____

_____

_____

What did you like to do together?

_____

_____

_____

Who were your favorite instructors or professors, and why?

_____

_____

_____

If you didn't pursue a formal education, what was your training and experience?

_____

_____

_____

What was dating like when you were a young adult?

_____

_____

_____

What do you consider your occupation to be?

_____

_____

Do you feel like you "fell into" your career, or did it take a lot of planning?

_____

_____

What was your first professional job? How old were you, and how much did you make?

_____

_____

_____

Were you ever forced to make a big change in your career?

_____

_____

_____

What was it, and how did you overcome it?

_____

_____

_____

What was the most favorite job you've ever had? Why?

_____

_____

_____

What was the most lucrative job you've ever had?

_____

_____

_____

What was the worst job you've ever had? Why?

_____

_____

_____

_____

A Wild Night
Did you ever experience a wild night as a young adult? Describe it below.

_____

_____

_____

_____

_____

_____

_____

Holidays

What is your favorite holiday, and why?

_____

_____

_____

Did you have any special Halloween traditions with your child(ren)?

_____

_____

What is your favorite Halloween candy?

_____

Growing up, where did you usually spend the holidays, and with whom?

_____

_____

_____

When your children were growing up, where did you spend the holidays, and with whom?

_____

_____

_____

What are your favorite holiday dishes?

_____

_____

_____

What are your favorite parts of the holiday season?

_____

_____

_____

What are your favorite or most treasured holiday decorations?

_____

_____

_____

What are your favorite holiday songs?

_____

_____

_____

When you were growing up, how did your family celebrate Christmas or Hanukkah, and with whom?

_____

_____

When your children were growing up, how did your family celebrate Christmas or Hanukkah, and with whom?

_____

_____

Does your family have any special dishes it makes for Christmas or Hanukkah?

_____

_____

What was the most memorable New Year's Eve you ever spent?

_____

_____

What are your Easter or Passover traditions?

_____

_____

Are there any other holidays (religious or otherwise) that you regularly celebrated? How did you celebrate?

_____

_____

_____

A Favorite Recipe
Write your family's special holiday recipe here.

_____

_____

_____

_____

_____

For Future Generations

What You've Learned

What do you think are the most important things in life?

_____

_____

Is there an incident or a time in your life when you've felt blessed by extraordinary luck?

_____

_____

Is there anything people might not know about you, that you wish they knew?

_____

_____

Is there anything you wish you'd done differently in your life? What?

_____

_____

What issues do you wish people would care more about?

_____

_____

What do people get too riled up about?

_____

_____

What are the most important characteristics in a good friend?

_____

_____

What is the most important way you can be a good friend to others?

_____

_____

What is important to remember about family in general?

_____

_____

Do you have any hopes for future generations?

_____

_____

_____

How do you hope we will remember you?

_____

_____

_____

What do you love about our family?

_____

_____

_____

In what ways is the owner of this book similar to his or her parents? Different?

_____

_____

_____

_____

Paste a photo of us here.

Paternal Grandfather Interview

Name

_____

Likes and Dislikes

Favorite color

_____

Favorite animals

_____

Least favorite animals (or insects)

_____

Favorite food

_____

Favorite desserts

_____

Favorite snacks

_____

Favorite beverages

_____

Least favorite food and beverages

_____

Favorite movies

_____

_____

Favorite TV shows

_____

Favorite actors and actresses

_____

_____

Favorite authors and books

_____

_____

Favorite musicians or bands

_____

_____

Favorite season of the year

_____

Least favorite season of the year

_____

Your Parents

What were your parents' full names?

_____

_____

Where were your parents born and where did they grow up?

_____

_____

What is your family's ethnic background and where are your ancestors from?

_____

What languages were spoken in your home?

_____

How would you describe your mother?

_____

_____

_____

_____

How would you describe your father?

_____

_____

_____

Did your parents ever tell you any stories about growing up?

_____

_____

_____

_____

What recollections do you have about each of your grandparents?

_____

_____

_____

Do you remember your parents having particular interests or passions?

_____

What did your mother teach you about life?

_____

_____

What did your father teach you about life?

_____

_____

Religion and Spirituality

What is your religion?

_____

Did religion play a big part in your family's life growing up?

_____

_____

_____

What do you love the most about your place of worship?

_____

_____

_____

What aspects of your faith speak to you and impassion you the most?

_____

_____

Do you have a special prayer you often say?

_____

_____

Do you have a particular prayer you like to say before meals?

_____

_____

How has religion or spirituality enriched your life?

_____

_____

_____

What kind of advice would you give about your faith or spirituality?

_____

Favorite Religious Text
Do you have any favorite sacred passages? Write them below.

_____

_____

_____

_____

Your Best Stories

Write some of your favorite stories here.
What's the funniest thing that's ever happened to you?
Do you find yourself telling the same anecdote time and time again?

Pets

Are you a: ☐ cat person ☐ dog person ☐ fish person ☐ none ☐ other: _____

Do you think having a pet is important? Why or why not?

_____

_____

What is the oldest pet you've ever had?

_____

_____

Have you ever taught a pet any special tricks? Which pet and what were they?

_____

_____

List your favorite pets you've had.

Name   **Type of animal**

_____

Boy/Girl   Description

_____

Where did you get him/her?

_____

How old were you when you had him/her?

_____

Special recollections

_____

_____

_____

Name   **Type of animal**

_____

Boy/Girl   Description

_____

Where did you get him/her?

_____

How old were you when you had him/her?

_____

Special recollections

_____

_____

_____

Growing Up

What is the date of your birth? Where were you born?

_____

Do you know any stories about your birth?

_____
_____
_____

Where did you grow up?

_____

What are the names and birthdates of your brothers and sisters?

_____
_____
_____

Did you have a nickname? If so, how did you get it or who gave it to you?

_____
_____

Did you have any chores or family responsibilities? What were they?

_____
_____

Did you get an allowance? If so, how much?

_____
_____

Do you remember how you usually spent it?

_____
_____

How did you spend your summers as a child?

_____
_____

What did you usually do to celebrate your birthday?

_____
_____

Did you have any cousins or other relatives who were particularly special to you?

_____
_____

Do you have a memory of a favorite family trip or event?

_____
_____

Childhood Favorites

What was your favorite ice cream flavor?

_____

What was your favorite meal or snack?

_____
_____

What were some of your favorite childhood toys?

_____
_____
_____

What were your favorite books?

_____
_____
_____

What were your favorite TV or radio shows?

_____
_____
_____

What were your favorite movies?

_____
_____
_____

Who were your favorite celebrities?

_____
_____
_____

Who were your favorite musical performers?

_____
_____
_____

How did you listen to music?

_____
_____

Who were some of your best friends as a child?

_____
_____

What were your favorite games to play with friends?

_____
_____
_____

Teenage Years

What high school(s) did you attend?

_____

What did you like about high school?

_____

What did you dislike about high school?

_____

Which teachers made an impression on you, and why?

_____

How did you get to and from school?

_____

What after-school activities did you participate in?

_____

Did you have a job as a teenager? What did you do and how much were you paid?

_____

What did you do when you returned home from school?

_____

Who were some of your best friends as a teenager?

_____

What did you do when spending time with friends?

_____

What were some of the fashion fads of the time, and did you follow them?

_____

What kind of hairstyle did you have?

_____

What stores do you remember shopping at as a teen?

_____

Did you have any teenage rebellions?

_____

What were your favorite things to eat as a teenager?

_____

What were your favorite books?

_____

_____

What were some of your favorite movies?

_____

_____

What were some of your favorite TV or radio programs?

_____

_____

What were your favorite bands or musical performers?

_____

_____

Who were your favorite celebrities?

_____

_____

What were your favorite sports teams and who were your favorite athletes?

_____

_____

What were your hopes and fears about college or growing up?

_____

_____

When you graduated high school, did you feel like an adult?

_____

The Times

What is your generation called?

_____

What is the first major news event you remember hearing about as a child?

_____

What is a new invention or technology you remember seeing for the first time when you were young?

_____

How much did a movie ticket cost?

_____

Gallon of gas?   Burger and fries?

_____

Who was the first person you voted for president or other national office?

_____

What pivotal events in history do you remember happening, or did you witness firsthand?

_____

_____

College and Work

Where did you study after high school? When did you graduate, and what was your degree(s)?

_____

Who were your closest friends in college or as a young adult?

_____

_____

What did you like to do together?

_____

_____

Who were your favorite instructors or professors, and why?

_____

_____

_____

If you didn't pursue a formal education, what was your training and experience?

_____

_____

What was dating like when you were a young adult?

_____

_____

_____

What do you consider your occupation to be?

_____

Do you feel like you "fell into" your career, or did it take a lot of planning?

_____

_____

What was your first professional job? How old were you, and how much did you make?

_____

_____

_____

Were you ever forced to make a big change in your career?

_____

_____

_____

What was it, and how did you overcome it?

_____

_____

What was the most favorite job you've ever had? Why?

_____

_____

What was the most lucrative job you've ever had?

_____

_____

_____

What was the worst job you've ever had? Why?

_____

_____

_____

_____

A Wild Night
Did you ever experience a wild night as a young adult? Describe it below.

_____

_____

_____

_____

_____

_____

_____

_____

Holidays

What is your favorite holiday, and why?

_____
_____
_____

Did you have any special Halloween traditions with your child(ren)?

_____
_____

What is your favorite Halloween candy?

_____

Growing up, where did you usually spend the holidays, and with whom?

_____
_____

When your children were growing up, where did you spend the holidays, and with whom?

_____
_____
_____

What are your favorite holiday dishes?

_____
_____

What are your favorite parts of the holiday season?

_____
_____

What are your favorite or most treasured holiday decorations?

_____
_____

What are your favorite holiday songs?

_____
_____

When you were growing up, how did your family celebrate Christmas or Hanukkah, and with whom?

_____

_____

_____

When your children were growing up, how did your family celebrate Christmas or Hanukkah, and with whom?

_____

_____

_____

Does your family have any special dishes it makes for Christmas or Hanukkah?

_____

_____

_____

What was the most memorable New Year's Eve you ever spent?

_____

_____

_____

What are your Easter or Passover traditions?

_____

_____

_____

Are there any other holidays (religious or otherwise) that you regularly celebrated? How did you celebrate?

_____

_____

_____

A Favorite Tradition
Write your family's special holiday tradition here.

_____

_____

_____

_____

_____

_____

_____

For Future Generations

What You've Learned

What do you think are the most important things in life?

_____

_____

_____

Is there an incident or a time in your life when you've felt blessed by extraordinary luck?

_____

_____

Is there anything people might not know about you, that you wish they knew?

_____

_____

Is there anything you wish you'd done differently in your life? What?

_____

_____

What issues do you wish people would care more about?

_____

_____

What do people get too riled up about?

_____

_____

What are the most important characteristics in a good friend?

_____

_____

What is the most important way you can be a good friend to others?

_____

_____

_____

What is important to remember about family in general?

_____

_____

Do you have any hopes for future generations?

_____

_____

_____

How do you hope we will remember you?

_____

_____

_____

What do you love about our family?

_____

_____

In what ways is the owner of this book similar to his or her parents? Different?

_____

_____

_____

Paste a photo of us here.

Family Members
and Friends Interviews

There are so many people in our lives that give us the wonderful sense of family. From your loving aunt to the cousins that you have been inseparable from since childhood to the friends of the family that feel like part of the family.

Use this section of this special book to ask them questions and find out more about them.

Adding them to this keepsake will not only make them feel special, but it will give you a lasting memento of their thoughts and feelings about you and your family.

Family Members and Friends

What is your full name?

_____

How are you related to our family?

_____

What is your birthdate?

_____

Where were you born?

_____

Where did you attend college?

_____

If you're married, what was the date and location of your wedding?

_____

What do you remember most about your mother?

_____

_____

_____

What do you remember most about your father?

_____

_____

_____

_____

What do you remember most about each of your grandparents?

_____

_____

_____

_____

_____

What is one of your first memories of the owner of this book?

_____

_____

_____

_____

What is one of your favorite memories of the owner of this book?

_____

_____

_____

_____

In what ways are people in our family similar to his or her parents? Different?

_____

_____

_____

_____

What do you think are the most important things in life?

_____

_____

_____

_____

What are your hopes and dreams for the owner of this book?

_____

_____

_____

_____

Family Members and Friends

What is your full name?

_____

How are you related to our family?

_____

What is your birthdate?

_____

Where were you born?

_____

Where did you attend college?

_____

If you're married, what was the date and location of your wedding?

_____

What do you remember most about your mother?

_____

_____

What do you remember most about your father?

_____

_____

_____

What do you remember most about each of your grandparents?

_____

_____

_____

_____

What is one of your first memories of the owner of this book?

_____

_____

_____

What is one of your favorite memories of the owner of this book?

_____

_____

_____

In what ways are people in our family similar to his or her parents? Different?

_____

_____

_____

_____

What do you think are the most important things in life?

_____

_____

_____

_____

What are your hopes and dreams for the owner of this book?

_____

_____

_____

_____

Family Members and Friends

What is your full name?

_____

How are you related to our family?

_____

What is your birthdate?

_____

Where were you born?

_____

Where did you attend college?

_____

If you're married, what was the date and location of your wedding?

_____

What do you remember most about your mother?

_____

_____

What do you remember most about your father?

_____

_____

_____

What do you remember most about each of your grandparents?

_____

_____

_____

_____

_____

What is one of your first memories of the owner of this book?

_____

_____

_____

_____

What is one of your favorite memories of the owner of this book?

_____

_____

_____

_____

In what ways are people in our family similar to his or her parents? Different?

_____

_____

_____

_____

_____

What do you think are the most important things in life?

_____

_____

_____

_____

_____

What are your hopes and dreams for the owner of this book?

_____

_____

_____

_____

_____

Family Members and Friends

What is your full name?

_____

How are you related to our family?

_____

What is your birthdate?

_____

Where were you born?

_____

Where did you attend college?

_____

If you're married, what was the date and location of your wedding?

_____

What do you remember most about your mother?

_____

_____

What do you remember most about your father?

_____

_____

What do you remember most about each of your grandparents?

_____

_____

_____

What is one of your first memories of the owner of this book?

_____

_____

_____

_____

What is one of your favorite memories of the owner of this book?

_____

_____

_____

_____

In what ways are people in our family similar to his or her parents? Different?

_____

_____

_____

_____

What do you think are the most important things in life?

_____

_____

_____

_____

What are your hopes and dreams for the owner of this book?

_____

_____

_____

_____

_____

Family Members and Friends

What is your full name?

_____

How are you related to our family?

_____

What is your birthdate?

_____

Where were you born?

_____

Where did you attend college?

_____

If you're married, what was the date and location of your wedding?

_____

What do you remember most about your mother?

_____

_____

_____

What do you remember most about your father?

_____

_____

_____

What do you remember most about each of your grandparents?

_____

_____

_____

_____

What is one of your first memories of the owner of this book?

_____

_____

_____

What is one of your favorite memories of the owner of this book?

_____

_____

_____

In what ways are people in our family similar to his or her parents? Different?

_____

_____

_____

_____

What do you think are the most important things in life?

_____

_____

_____

_____

What are your hopes and dreams for the owner of this book?

_____

_____

_____

_____

Family Members and Friends

What is your full name?

_____

How are you related to our family?

_____

What is your birthdate?

_____

Where were you born?

_____

Where did you attend college?

_____

If you're married, what was the date and location of your wedding?

_____

What do you remember most about your mother?

_____

_____

_____

What do you remember most about your father?

_____

_____

_____

_____

What do you remember most about each of your grandparents?

_____

_____

_____

_____

_____

What is one of your first memories of the owner of this book?

_____
_____
_____

What is one of your favorite memories of the owner of this book?

_____
_____
_____

In what ways are people in our family similar to his or her parents? Different?

_____
_____
_____
_____

What do you think are the most important things in life?

_____
_____
_____
_____

What are your hopes and dreams for the owner of this book?

_____
_____
_____
_____

Family Members and Friends

What is your full name?

_____

How are you related to our family?

_____

What is your birthdate?

_____

Where were you born?

_____

Where did you attend college?

_____

If you're married, what was the date and location of your wedding?

_____

What do you remember most about your mother?

_____

_____

What do you remember most about your father?

_____

_____

_____

What do you remember most about each of your grandparents?

_____

_____

_____

_____

_____

What is one of your first memories of the owner of this book?

_____
_____
_____
_____

What is one of your favorite memories of the owner of this book?

_____
_____
_____
_____

In what ways are people in our family similar to his or her parents? Different?

_____
_____
_____
_____

What do you think are the most important things in life?

_____
_____
_____
_____

What are your hopes and dreams for the owner of this book?

_____
_____
_____
_____

Family Members and Friends

What is your full name?

_____

How are you related to our family?

_____

What is your birthdate?

_____

Where were you born?

_____

Where did you attend college?

_____

If you're married, what was the date and location of your wedding?

_____

What do you remember most about your mother?

_____

_____

What do you remember most about your father?

_____

_____

_____

What do you remember most about each of your grandparents?

_____

_____

_____

_____

_____

What is one of your first memories of the owner of this book?

_____

_____

_____

_____

What is one of your favorite memories of the owner of this book?

_____

_____

_____

_____

In what ways are people in our family similar to his or her parents? Different?

_____

_____

_____

_____

What do you think are the most important things in life?

_____

_____

_____

_____

What are your hopes and dreams for the owner of this book?

_____

_____

_____

_____

Family Members and Friends

What is your full name?

_____

How are you related to our family?

_____

What is your birthdate?

_____

Where were you born?

_____

Where did you attend college?

_____

If you're married, what was the date and location of your wedding?

_____

What do you remember most about your mother?

_____

_____

What do you remember most about your father?

_____

_____

_____

What do you remember most about each of your grandparents?

_____

_____

_____

_____

_____

What is one of your first memories of the owner of this book?

_____

_____

_____

_____

What is one of your favorite memories of the owner of this book?

_____

_____

_____

_____

In what ways are people in our family similar to his or her parents? Different?

_____

_____

_____

_____

What do you think are the most important things in life?

_____

_____

_____

_____

What are your hopes and dreams for the owner of this book?

_____

_____

_____

_____

Family Members and Friends

What is your full name?

_____

How are you related to our family?

_____

What is your birthdate?

_____

Where were you born?

_____

Where did you attend college?

_____

If you're married, what was the date and location of your wedding?

_____

What do you remember most about your mother?

_____

_____

What do you remember most about your father?

_____

_____

_____

What do you remember most about each of your grandparents?

_____

_____

_____

_____

_____

What is one of your first memories of the owner of this book?

_____

_____

_____

_____

What is one of your favorite memories of the owner of this book?

_____

_____

_____

_____

In what ways are people in our family similar to his or her parents? Different?

_____

_____

_____

_____

What do you think are the most important things in life?

_____

_____

_____

_____

What are your hopes and dreams for the owner of this book?

_____

_____

_____

_____

Family Members and Friends

What is your full name?

_____

How are you related to our family?

_____

What is your birthdate?

_____

Where were you born?

_____

Where did you attend college?

_____

If you're married, what was the date and location of your wedding?

_____

What do you remember most about your mother?

_____

_____

What do you remember most about your father?

_____

_____

_____

What do you remember most about each of your grandparents?

_____

_____

_____

_____

What is one of your first memories of the owner of this book?

_____

_____

_____

What is one of your favorite memories of the owner of this book?

_____

_____

_____

In what ways are people in our family similar to his or her parents? Different?

_____

_____

_____

_____

What do you think are the most important things in life?

_____

_____

_____

_____

What are your hopes and dreams for the owner of this book?

_____

_____

_____

_____

_____

Family Members and Friends

What is your full name?

_____

How are you related to our family?

_____

What is your birthdate?

_____

Where were you born?

_____

Where did you attend college?

_____

If you're married, what was the date and location of your wedding?

_____

What do you remember most about your mother?

_____

_____

_____

What do you remember most about your father?

_____

_____

_____

What do you remember most about each of your grandparents?

_____

_____

_____

_____

What is one of your first memories of the owner of this book?

_____

_____

_____

_____

What is one of your favorite memories of the owner of this book?

_____

_____

_____

_____

In what ways are people in our family similar to his or her parents? Different?

_____

_____

_____

_____

_____

What do you think are the most important things in life?

_____

_____

_____

_____

What are your hopes and dreams for the owner of this book?

_____

_____

_____

_____

_____

Family Members and Friends

What is your full name?

_____

How are you related to our family?

_____

What is your birthdate?

_____

Where were you born?

_____

Where did you attend college?

_____

If you're married, what was the date and location of your wedding?

_____

What do you remember most about your mother?

_____

_____

_____

What do you remember most about your father?

_____

_____

_____

What do you remember most about each of your grandparents?

_____

_____

_____

_____

What is one of your first memories of the owner of this book?

_____
_____
_____
_____

What is one of your favorite memories of the owner of this book?

_____
_____
_____
_____

In what ways are people in our family similar to his or her parents? Different?

_____
_____
_____
_____

What do you think are the most important things in life?

_____
_____
_____
_____

What are your hopes and dreams for the owner of this book?

_____
_____
_____
_____
_____

Family Members and Friends

What is your full name?

_____

How are you related to our family?

_____

What is your birthdate?

_____

Where were you born?

_____

Where did you attend college?

_____

If you're married, what was the date and location of your wedding?

_____

What do you remember most about your mother?

_____

_____

_____

What do you remember most about your father?

_____

_____

_____

What do you remember most about each of your grandparents?

_____

_____

_____

_____

_____

What is one of your first memories of the owner of this book?

_____

_____

_____

_____

What is one of your favorite memories of the owner of this book?

_____

_____

_____

_____

In what ways are people in our family similar to his or her parents? Different?

_____

_____

_____

_____

What do you think are the most important things in life?

_____

_____

_____

_____

What are your hopes and dreams for the owner of this book?

_____

_____

_____

_____

Family Members and Friends

What is your full name?

_____

How are you related to our family?

_____

What is your birthdate?

_____

Where were you born?

_____

Where did you attend college?

_____

If you're married, what was the date and location of your wedding?

_____

What do you remember most about your mother?

_____

_____

What do you remember most about your father?

_____

_____

_____

What do you remember most about each of your grandparents?

_____

_____

_____

_____

_____

What is one of your first memories of the owner of this book?

_____

_____

_____

_____

What is one of your favorite memories of the owner of this book?

_____

_____

_____

_____

In what ways are people in our family similar to his or her parents? Different?

_____

_____

_____

_____

What do you think are the most important things in life?

_____

_____

_____

_____

What are your hopes and dreams for the owner of this book?

_____

_____

_____

_____

Family Members and Friends

What is your full name?

_____

How are you related to our family?

_____

What is your birthdate?

_____

Where were you born?

_____

Where did you attend college?

_____

If you're married, what was the date and location of your wedding?

_____

What do you remember most about your mother?

_____

_____

_____

What do you remember most about your father?

_____

_____

_____

_____

What do you remember most about each of your grandparents?

_____

_____

_____

_____

_____

What is one of your first memories of the owner of this book?

_____

_____

_____

_____

What is one of your favorite memories of the owner of this book?

_____

_____

_____

_____

In what ways are people in our family similar to his or her parents? Different?

_____

_____

_____

_____

What do you think are the most important things in life?

_____

_____

_____

_____

What are your hopes and dreams for the owner of this book?

_____

_____

_____

_____

_____

Family Members and Friends

What is your full name?

_____

How are you related to our family?

_____

What is your birthdate?

_____

Where were you born?

_____

Where did you attend college?

_____

If you're married, what was the date and location of your wedding?

_____

What do you remember most about your mother?

_____

_____

_____

What do you remember most about your father?

_____

_____

_____

_____

What do you remember most about each of your grandparents?

_____

_____

_____

_____

What is one of your first memories of the owner of this book?

_____

_____

_____

_____

What is one of your favorite memories of the owner of this book?

_____

_____

_____

_____

In what ways are people in our family similar to his or her parents? Different?

_____

_____

_____

_____

What do you think are the most important things in life?

_____

_____

_____

_____

What are your hopes and dreams for the owner of this book?

_____

_____

_____

_____

_____

Family Members and Friends

What is your full name?

_____

How are you related to our family?

_____

What is your birthdate?

_____

Where were you born?

_____

Where did you attend college?

_____

If you're married, what was the date and location of your wedding?

_____

What do you remember most about your mother?

_____

_____

What do you remember most about your father?

_____

_____

_____

What do you remember most about each of your grandparents?

_____

_____

_____

_____

_____

What is one of your first memories of the owner of this book?

_____

_____

_____

What is one of your favorite memories of the owner of this book?

_____

_____

_____

In what ways are people in our family similar to his or her parents? Different?

_____

_____

_____

_____

What do you think are the most important things in life?

_____

_____

_____

_____

What are your hopes and dreams for the owner of this book?

_____

_____

_____

_____